essentia

Leading Teams

Time-saving books that teach specific skills to busy people, focusing on what really matters; the things that make a difference – the *essentials*. Other books in the series include:

Making Great Presentations

Coaching People

Responding to Stress

Succeeding at Interviews

Solving Problems

Hiring People

Getting Started on the Internet

Writing Great Copy

Making the Best Man's Speech

Writing Good Reports

Feeling Good for No Good Reason

Making the Most of Your Time

For full details please send for a free copy of the latest catalogue. See back cover for address.

The things that really matter about

Leading
Teams

Rob Yeung

ESSENTIALS

First published in 2000 by
How To Books Ltd, 3 Newtec Place,
Magdalen Road, Oxford OX4 1RE, United Kingdom
Tel: (01865) 793806   Fax: (01865) 248780
email: info@howtobooks.co.uk
www.howtobooks.co.uk

British Library Cataloguing in Publication Data.
A catalogue record for this book is available from
the British Library.

Edited by Diana Brueton
Cover design by Shireen Nathoo Designs
Produced for How To Books by Deer Park Productions
Cover copy by Sallyann Sheridan
Typeset by Anneset, Weston-super-Mare, Somerset
Printed and bound by Hillman Printers, Frome, Somerset

NOTE: The material contained in this book is set out in good faith for
general guidance and no liability can be accepted for loss or expense
incurred as a result of relying in particular circumstances on
statements made in the book. Laws and regulations are complex and
liable to change, and readers should check the current position with
the relevant authorities before making personal arrangements.

ESSENTIALS *is an imprint of*
How To Books

Contents

Preface

A team of people is greater than the sum of its parts – a fact that is recognised in organisations across the world. However, effective teamworking doesn't just happen on its own – individuals have to be taught how to work together and motivated to achieve results. This book is written for those who find themselves leading teams.

Whether you're a first-time supervisor or a long-serving senior manager, the principles are the same. Leaders must create a common purpose for the members of the team and support them, develop them, and guide them through conflict to achieve that purpose. Whether you are setting up a new team or working with an existing team, you can apply these principles to turn any collection of individuals into a team of highly committed people who enjoy working together.

While the traditional style of managing teams is based on barking orders at members of the team and leaving them to it, *leading* teams focuses on harnessing the creativity and skills of the people in a team so that everyone can enjoy the work at hand. This book gives you the essentials of leading teams – what really matters if you want to **lead your team successfully and get results**.

Rob Yeung

1 Learning the Essentials

To achieve more than the sum of its parts, a team needs a shared goal and the right people.

4

things that
really matter

1 **UNDERSTANDING THE NEED FOR TEAMS**

2 **DIFFERENTIATING TEAMS FROM GROUPS**

3 **SETTING AN OBJECTIVE**

4 **SELECTING TEAM MEMBERS**

We all hear about the need to work in teams – but what's all the fuss about? In order to lead a team effectively, you need to first understand the benefits of getting a group of individuals to work together as a team.

However, **teams differ from mere groups** of individuals. A team has a **common purpose and goals** that must be agreed upon by all members of the team. Your first job as team leader – even before you start to assemble your team – is to formulate a clear picture in your own mind of what you need the team to do. You might have a task to accomplish, but why do you need a team exactly? What is your **objective**?

If you are fortunate enough to be able to put together a team from scratch, first ask yourself what **skills** you will need on the team to meet your stated objective.

Understanding the basics of teams is the first step to assembling and building an effective team.

IS THIS YOU?

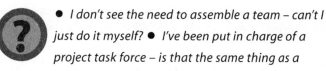

● *I don't see the need to assemble a team – can't I just do it myself?* ● *I've been put in charge of a project task force – is that the same thing as a team?* ● *I don't know whether we're a real team or just a collection of people – a group – who work together.* ● *I've been told that groups eventually become teams anyway, so why should I bother to lead it?* ● *I have to put a project team together to research a new product but I don't know where to begin.* ● *I don't have a clue what skills I need for my team.* ● *We don't have the right people for the team – should we ask an external consultant to joint us?* ● *I think Jane has the analytical skills I need for our team. Now I just need to persuade her to join the team.*

UNDERSTANDING THE NEED FOR TEAMS

More and more organisations are encouraging people to work together in teams – and there are good reasons for doing so. Teams of people working effectively together can:

- Achieve a better result than the individuals working alone – 'the whole is greater than the sum of its parts'.

- Get more done in less time than individuals alone.

- Work to the strengths of individuals, while compensating for the weaknesses of others.

- Split the work up amongst members of the team and make a task seem less daunting.

So it's hardly surprising that teams exist in almost every organisation in the world. What unites teams is the fact that they allow people to work together more effectively than the individuals would be able to alone. Teams are especially useful in the following situations:

- When no one person has the skills, ideas, experience, or time needed to tackle a particular problem, task, or issue.

- When you or the organisation is faced with a problem or issue that no one has an answer for yet.

- When time is short – for example when you're going through rapid organisational change.

- When a group of people need to collaborate closely to get things done.

Do you fit one of the above criteria? If the answer is yes, you definitely need a team. If the answer is no, you might need to think again or consult a colleague as to whether you need a team or not.

There are many different types of teams, but they all allow people to work together more effectively to get things done.

 DIFFERENTIATING TEAMS FROM GROUPS

When people think of teams, they often think of sports teams. Teams in the workplace can bear little similarity to sports teams, so it can be natural to wonder whether you are a real team or not. How can you tell whether you work in a team or are simply a group of individuals?

There are many different types of teams. The following is by no means a definitive list:

- project teams

- customer service teams
- sales teams
- work groups
- management teams
- cross-functional teams
- product development teams
- task forces
- top teams.

So some teams, it seems, aren't even called 'teams'! The key criterion is that if the members of your group **share at least one goal** and depend on each other to succeed, then you're a team. So, for example, a collection of people who sit together in an open-plan office but who work on different projects is not a team. Even a group of people who work on similar projects may not be a team if, for example, they do not depend on the success or failure of each other. However, a group of people who are based in offices across the length and breadth of the country – but are working on the same project – are a team.

While some people believe that groups will naturally become teams, this simply does not happen on its own! Teams can achieve much more than groups, but **putting together a team requires leadership** in the first instance to define an objective – and that's your job.

Geography and titles don't matter. As long as you have a shared goal, you're a team.

 SETTING AN OBJECTIVE

You may decide that you need to put a team together to do a particular piece of work. Someone else in your organisation may ask you to put a team together to tackle a specific problem. Or you may have been put in charge of an existing team. But before you can start thinking about who should or should not be on your team, you must establish what it is that you want the team to achieve. **What is the purpose of your team?**

Only when you have a good idea of what you need to achieve can you begin to select the people best suited to help you reach your **objective**. It might help to ask yourself the following questions:

- What do we need to achieve?

- When do we need to achieve it by?

- What knowledge, skills or experience do we need on the team?

- What resources or budget do we have?

- What will happen if the team fails to achieve its objective?

While a group can have a loosely defined purpose or none at all, a team must have an objective that it intends to achieve.

 SELECTING TEAM MEMBERS

Now that you know the kind of skills that you need to achieve your objective, you have to find the most appropriate people to help you. While you may know some of the people you need, you may identify some skills or experience that you need but not know of a person with that skill. But just because you don't personally know of an individual with a particular skill doesn't mean that he or she does not exist!

The answer is to **network** or ask around within your organisation:

- Tell your immediate colleagues – your **first contacts** – the sort of skills or experience that you are looking for.

- Ask them to come up with suggestions of people who might fit the bill.

- If they don't know anyone who might be right, ask them if they know other people – your **second contacts** – with whom you could get in touch.

- Then ask those second contacts for names of people who might have the skills you are looking for.

- If they don't know, go to your **third contacts**, and so on. Eventually (hopefully), you should find the right person for the job.

Don't be surprised if prospective team members are a little reticent to join up! Working on a cross-functional team or a project team can involve a lot of effort and hard work. So you might need to use your influencing skills to **persuade** the people you want to join your team.

When you do approach a prospective team member, try to:

- Explain the purpose of the team.

- Spell out what you think they can contribute to the team.

- Point out the benefit to them of working on the team.

- Listen to their objections and try to find reasonable arguments that will overcome those objections.

- Give them the opportunity not to join the team. For

example, they may be too busy with other work. If you are more senior than a prospective team member, try to avoid using your authority to intimidate someone into joining the team!

Don't force people to join your team. If they aren't fully committed, they will never add much value to the team.

There may be occasions when no one within your organisation has the skills or time to help. In such situations you may need to bring in external **consultants** to help you achieve your objectives. If you think you need to use consultants, make sure that you:

- Ask your colleagues for personal recommendations of consultants they have worked successfully with in the area that you need help with.

- Meet with the consultants to make sure that you would feel comfortable working with them.

- Get them to write a proposal so that you can see exactly what they are promising to do and how much it will cost.

- Don't treat consultants as enemies. Once you have decided to use a particular consultant or group of consultants, treat them as equal team members.

Consultants can bring valuable skills to the mix, but can be costly. So always make sure you know why you are using them.

MAKING WHAT MATTERS WORK FOR YOU

✔ Understand that effective teams can produce results that individuals working alone could never dream of! However, don't assemble a team unless you're sure you actually need one.

✔ Remember that teams come in many guises and forms – and some of them aren't even called 'teams'! It's not about geography or titles, it's about having a common purpose – an objective – that bonds all the members of the team.

✔ Be absolutely clear why you are assembling a team and what skills or resources you will need for your team.

✔ Try to find people within the organisation with the skills you need. Only if you are sure that no one within your organisation can help you meet your objective should you bring in an external consultant.

2 Creating a Team

High performing teams do not happen by magic. They are assembled and nurtured from the start.

4

things that
really matter

1 **UNDERSTANDING HOW TEAMS DEVELOP**

2 **PLANNING YOUR MEETING SPACE**

3 **HANDLING THE TEAM KICK-OFF**

4 **GETTING TO KNOW EACH OTHER**

Simply bringing together a collection of people does not ensure that they will work together effectively. Understanding how **teams develop** will help you to **plan** and **manage difficulties** within the team. Team members need time to test each other out and learn about the best ways of dealing with each other to enable the team to **perform** together as quickly as possible.

In particular, the first time your team members meet requires careful handling. First, as the team leader, you have to be **prepared** and appear **competent**. The meeting place that you choose is an often overlooked part of the preparation. And if your team members have never met before, you may need to **break the ice** as the first step to help them get to know each other and understand what they can bring to the team.

Great teams don't just 'happen' – they require forethought and planning.

IS THIS YOU?

- *I've got my team members together – now what?*
- *I've heard that teams go through stages of development, but I'm not sure what the stages are!*
- *Although I have a little experience of supervising a team, I really want to get it right with this new team.* ● *I never seem to know what preparation I can do before team meetings.* ● *I need to introduce the team members to each other but I want to do it in a different way from the usual!* ● *No one ever reads minutes from the meetings, but what's the alternative?*
- *People turning up late for meetings always frustrate me. I want to put a stop to it if I can.* ● *I've been in meetings where no one wanted to talk to each other and no one knew why they were there. I don't want to repeat that nightmare.*

UNDERSTANDING HOW TEAMS DEVELOP

Putting a group of people together in a room is not enough to get them working together as a team. It takes time for people to get to know each other and become comfortable working together. However, by understanding the **stages** that a team goes through when it works together, you can **accelerate** the process.

A team may not automatically progress from one stage to the next, but you can ensure that it does.

Different teams take different lengths of time to move from one stage to the next and **some teams can get stuck** in a particular stage. However, most teams move through the following five stages:

- **Forming.** When a team first gets together members may not know each other very well and take gentle steps to find out more about each other. They may treat each other politely and be quite guarded about what they say or do. Some people may say quite a lot and seem enthusiastic; others may say almost nothing. At this point, not much work will get done.

- **Storming.** Members of the team start testing each other out more vigorously, trying to find out each others' strengths and weaknesses. There is a lot more discussion, as well as frequent conflict and clashes, as people begin to figure out where they sit within the team. At this point the team may start to get some work done.

- **Norming.** The team members now know each other fairly well and norms or standards are developing in terms of how people treat each other. For instance, norms may develop around how open members are with each other or the language or jargon that they use. Some real work is being done but norming is still only the precursor to the next stage.

- **Performing.** Finally, the team knows how to play to the strengths and compensate for the weaknesses of its members. Meetings are lively, but there are few clashes. Team members are supportive of each other and will bend over backwards to help each other achieve the goals that have been set. Only now is the team fully engaged with the task at hand.

- **Mourning.** When a project or task has been completed, it is time to celebrate what the team has achieved and prepare to move on to new challenges. The team may experience feelings of sadness at having to break up, but it is time to tie up loose ends and prepare to join new teams.

Understanding the different stages will help you move the team from forming through to performing as quickly as possible.

 PLANNING YOUR MEETING SPACE

In so many meetings people sit around a round or long table with the chairperson or leader of the team at the head of it, while another team member takes notes or minutes. Unfortunately, this is neither exciting for team members nor effective. So why not **do something different** if you can?

For the best results, try to find the following for your first team meeting:

- A room where you can move the furniture around. Can you **set up the tables to form the shape of a U**? If you can, put the chairs behind the U so that everyone looks inwards towards the centre of the U. Then you ,as team leader, can walk about the room, providing team members with a moving focus of attention to help keep them from falling asleep!

- Two **flip chart stands** and lots of **flip chart paper** (and thick pens for writing on the flip chart) for you to write on. Put the flip charts at the front of the room, at the 'opening' of the U-shaped table arrangement. The problem with taking minutes is that no one can see them until after they have been typed up and distributed. Writing notes up on a flip chart during the course of a meeting allows everyone to see the notes that have been taken.

- **Masking tape or Blu-tack**. Once you have completed writing on one sheet of paper, tear it off the flip chart stand and use the masking tape or Blu-tack to put it up on a wall. In this way the team can always refer back to what was discussed earlier.

Think laterally about other tools that you could use to make meetings more effective. Don't be constrained by pen and paper techniques. Use whatever works for your team.

HANDLING THE TEAM KICK-OFF

Now it's your first team meeting. Unfortunately, while a few people may know each other fairly well, others may never have met – this is the **forming stage**. You need to use an **icebreaker** to help the team move past forming as quickly as possible.

Rather than asking team members to describe themselves, try asking them to **draw pictures** that describe themselves! After you have welcomed everyone to the first meeting and briefly re-described the purpose of the team:

- Explain that the first task is to help members learn a bit about each other. It's a light-hearted – yet effective – way of breaking the ice.

- Give them each a sheet of flip chart paper and a selection of coloured flip chart pens.

- Then explain that you want them to draw a picture that represents their lives. It's not a picture of what they look like – it's a picture that tries to convey not only what they do within the organisation but also a little about their hobbies and lives outside of work. The only rule is that no one is allowed to use words in their pictures!

- Give them about five minutes to draw their pictures, then ask each member of the team to show his or her picture to the rest of the team and spend just a few minutes explaining the different parts of the picture.

There are dozens of ways to break the ice. Ask your colleagues what icebreakers they have experienced and how well it broke the ice for the teams that they were on.

The next task is to establish some **ground rules** as to how the team is going to behave towards each other. Forcing the group to think about ground rules helps to save time on the **storming** stage.

Ask the team to discuss the following questions and come up with answers that everyone agrees with:

- What is the purpose of our team? What is our team 'mission statement'?

- Is the size of the team fixed? How are we going to decide to bring new people on to the team? How will we remove or replace members of the team?

- Do we need our activities to be secret? How much of the content of our meetings are we allowed to talk to our colleagues about?

- How often should we meet and for how long?

- Are we going to allow members to receive incoming calls on their mobiles during meetings or not?

- How should we deal with people who miss or are late for meetings?

- What other ground rules do we need to agree upon?

- How are we going to deal with people who break the ground rules? Do we need a system of forfeits, such as having to make everyone cups of tea?

Once the team has decided on a set of ground rules, these should be written up on flip charts or perhaps typed and circulated amongst the team.

Ground rules are there to help the team meet its objectives. Apply them with as much authority or flexibility as your team requires – don't follow them slavishly if they are stopping the team from working effectively.

 GETTING TO KNOW EACH OTHER

Another key step to help the team move past the forming stage is to encourage people to **talk about themselves** in a little more detail.

It might be worth preparing a list of questions on a sheet of flip chart paper before the meeting to encourage people to share some information about themselves with each other. Give the team some time to think about the answers, then ask them to share their answers with the rest of the team:

- What is your greatest strength?

- What is your greatest weakness?

- What do you enjoy most about working in a team?

- What do you find most irritating or frustrating about working with other people?

- What experience or skills do you bring to the team?

- What would you like to learn from working on the team?

You should also ask the team what other questions they would like to ask each other. If you want to make the task a little more fun, you could also add an item such as 'Tell the team something about yourself that no one in the room knows about you' – the answers will at least usually bring a smile to people's faces!

*You may not achieve much tangible work in your first meeting, but don't worry. Getting people to know each other is a vital step on the way to helping the team reach the **performing** stage.*

Team meetings can be rather formal affairs. Often, the best way to help people get to know each other is to give them the opportunity to relax, chat to each other informally, and have fun. Wherever possible try to arrange for the team to have lunch, dinner or just drinks together out of the office. Arrange a trip to go bowling or perhaps play football in a local park. Use your imagination to come up with a fun way for people to **bond**. Having a laugh is a great way to break the ice.

MAKING WHAT MATTERS WORK FOR YOU

✔ Recognise that teams are made up of people who need time to get to know each other before they can get to grips with working together effectively. Understanding the five stages of team development will help you to manage a team to achieve results in the shortest possible time.

✔ Use the layout of the room and tools of the trade to make the most effective use of meetings.

✔ Break the ice in a light-hearted fashion. Meetings don't all have to be serious and boring. Drawing a picture is an effective yet fun way of helping the group through the forming stage.

✔ Help the members of the team to speed through the process of getting to know each other. Formal question and answer sessions can play a part. However, informal gatherings also help team members become more comfortable with each other.

3 Making a Team Work

Defining, refining, and agreeing actions lies at the heart of effective teamworking.

6

things that really matter

1 **DEFINING THE ISSUE**

2 **BRAINSTORMING IDEAS**

3 **EVALUATING OPTIONS**

4 **GATHERING INFORMATION**

5 **AGREEING ACTIONS**

6 **MEASURING RESULTS**

Whether you have put together a new team or are working with an existing team, you will need to agree in greater detail on **what the team is supposed to be doing** and **how it should do it**. This may take many meetings over the course of weeks or even months – but this is the start of the **teamworking process**.

But it's all very well to talk about what needs to happen. At some point the individual members of the team have to **take some responsibility** for going and getting things done.

Finally, the team needs to **measure and review its output** – did everyone achieve what they set out to do? If not, the team needs to take action to **rectify** the situation and ensure that it does not fall behind schedule again.

Involving the team in decision-making ensures that everyone is committed to the team's work.

IS THIS YOU?

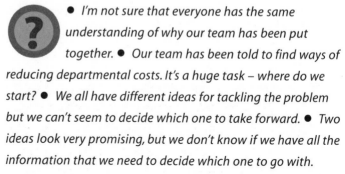

● I'm not sure that everyone has the same understanding of why our team has been put together. ● Our team has been told to find ways of reducing departmental costs. It's a huge task – where do we start? ● We all have different ideas for tackling the problem but we can't seem to decide which one to take forward. ● Two ideas look very promising, but we don't know if we have all the information that we need to decide which one to go with.

● We spend lots of time discussing things, but nothing ever seems to happen as a result of our meetings. ● We can't decide which option to go with, but we have a deadline in three weeks – we need to make a decision once and for all!

● My team is faced with a huge task – how do we break it down into more manageable chunks? ● The team seems a bit demoralised because we don't know how we're doing.

 ### DEFINING THE ISSUE

While you as the team leader may have a good idea of the purpose of the team, you need to make sure that everyone has the same understanding as you. Effort is often wasted because individuals have different ideas of why the team exists. Whether your team was set up to tackle a particular project or exists to provide ongoing services, it needs to agree on a **team mission statement**.

Having a clear team mission statement will help to channel the **enthusiasm and energy** of all of the team members.

You could try the following steps to create the team mission statement:

● Try to **inspire** the team with what you know of the

team's purpose. Tell the team why you think it was put together and present all the background information you have. If someone else is sponsoring the team, perhaps you could invite him or her along to the team meeting to speak and answer questions.

- Ask team members to **debate** the issue. The idea is not to think of ways of tackling it at the moment – you are just trying to get everyone to agree why they are all there.

- Finally try to help the team come up with a **single, unambiguous phrase** or a couple of sentences that encapsulate the purpose of the team.

- Check that **everyone agrees** with both the meaning and wording of the team mission statement.

- Keep a **copy of the team mission statement** at hand at subsequent meetings. This will help you to keep team discussions focused on its stated mission.

Examples of team mission statements include:

- To research and develop a new product by the end of the financial year.

- To raise £200,000 for research into the prevention of childhood diseases within 18 months.

- To provide ongoing professional and friendly support to customers who telephone our helpline for assistance.

- To organise a celebration of the company's 200th anniversary.

Mission statements should express worthy goals in a clear fashion that all of the members of the team can agree with.

BRAINSTORMING IDEAS

Once you have established what the team's mission or purpose is, it's time to ask: How are we going to achieve it?

Brainstorming is one of the most commonly used techniques for **encouraging creativity** and generating lots of ideas as to how to tackle a goal. The aim of brainstorming is to generate as many ideas as possible by deferring judgement as to the quality of each idea until after all the ideas have been written up. The reason for doing this is because – in many cases – the best idea for tackling a problem can often be the most supposedly 'obvious' idea or a 'silly' idea.

While most people have heard of brainstorming, many people actually fail to follow the **rules**, with the consequence that it does not generate as many ideas as it should. There are only two rules to brainstorming:

- **Every idea is recorded** – no idea is a 'bad', 'obvious', or 'silly' idea.

- **No idea is evaluated** during the brainstorming. Evaluation of the appropriateness of each idea happens only as the next step when the brainstorming has ended.

Brainstorming is about quantity first and quality later.

Brainstorming should be fun, with team members shouting out whatever ideas come into their heads, no matter how unfeasible or difficult they may be to put into practice. The only person not to contribute ideas should be yourself or whoever you choose to write up the suggestions as they are called out.

Make sure that there really is no evaluation – whether

verbal or not. For example, sighs, laughter, or shakes of the head are non-verbal ways for people to express their disapproval of ideas and are therefore banned during brainstorming!

You could follow these steps to effective brainstorming:

- Explain the rules of brainstorming. Even if team members are already familiar with the technique, it is still worth reiterating that the initial brainstorming process is about generating lots of ideas without evaluating any of them at all.

- Pose the question that is facing the team and ask people to shout out their ideas.

- Write all suggestions up on the flip chart. If people start calling out ideas too quickly, ask them to slow down so that you can capture all the suggestions.

- Keep encouraging people to think of suggestions. Remind them that they should just call out any ideas that come to mind – no matter how silly they might seem. At the same time remind people not to evaluate ideas – be polite but firm here!

- Carry on encouraging the team to come up with suggestions – even when the team seems to dry up. With a little persuasion, most people can create a few more ideas.

- When the group has finished, thank the team for their contributions.

 EVALUATING OPTIONS

Generating ideas should be relatively straightforward. However, the team now needs to decide which ideas to follow up – this is when it is time to **evaluate the ideas** that have been generated.

The **three-step process** is one way of cutting down the number of options and thinking about each of the ideas in a little more detail. The first two steps can be relatively quick, but the third step almost always takes a lot of time.

- **Discard impossible ideas.** Read out the list of ideas, one at a time. Tell team members to call out if anyone thinks that an idea is not possible or not relevant to the current situation. Cross out the idea unless anyone else in the team disagrees.

- **Eliminate duplication.** Ask the group to look at the entire list and cross out any ideas that are very closely linked.

- **List pros and cons.** Go through the list asking the team to think of the positive and negative points associated with each of the ideas. Write all of these up.

The three-step process is just one example of how to evaluate the list of ideas. Adapt it to work for you and your team.

 GATHERING INFORMATION

You may still, at this stage, have a half-dozen or more ideas. At some stage you will need to decide which **single option** to take forward. However, it may be premature to choose the single option. For example, the team may not have all the data it needs to make a rational decision, or several options may look equally promising for the moment. Consequently, you will have to help the team **gather information** on the top-rated options.

We think that moving our head office out of London will be the best way of cutting our property costs. However, we don't yet know how much rent is elsewhere.

The following questions may help you in assisting the team to gather the information it needs:

- What further information do we need to find out?

- If the information exists, who can provide us with the information or tell us where we can get it?

- If the information doesn't exist or we can't find it, how can we get a good estimate instead?

- Who on the team is the best person to find that information?

- How long will it take to get that information?

By the end of the meeting, you should have decided **who** on the team is going to find out **what** information. Ideally, the next time the team comes together for a meeting, everyone who needed to should have gathered the information.

Information is vital for making an informed choice.

 AGREEING ACTIONS

Now that the team has gathered all the information that it needs, the team will have to discuss how the various ideas compare with each other. The eventual aim is to decide what **course of action** to take.

To help the discussion, you could use questions such as:

- Now that we have more information, are there any

options that we can eliminate because they are too costly, time-consuming or difficult to do?

- Which option do we prefer?

- Why do you prefer option X to option Y?

- Have we overlooked any options?

Hopefully, the team will be able to debate the various options and choose the one to follow. However, it is often the case that teams can get **stuck** in heated arguments over the relative merits and demerits of various options. If this is the case you may need to **force a decision** – especially, for example, if you have a deadline to meet. There are various ways for you to help your team make a decision, such as:

- **Open voting**. Begin by telling the team what the 'rules' of the vote are. For example, will the decision be made simply on the basis of which option gets the most votes? Or will the voting be used to identify the top two or three options for further discussion? Whatever rules you adopt, you must check with the team that they all agree to **abide** by the outcome of the vote. When actually taking the vote, ask each person in turn to call out his or her number one choice. When everyone (including yourself) has voted, total up the votes and announce the 'winning' option.

- **Secret ballot**. Sometimes, when there is a very senior or dominating person on a team, his or her vote can sway the decisions of others. In order to prevent this, you could ask people to write down their choices on pieces of paper. You can then collect the pieces of paper and announce the option to be taken forward.

Whatever the outcome, it is important to check that all the members of the team agree with the single option and are **committed** to it. Very often people who feel that the decision did not go their way put in less effort than those who do agree with the chosen option. It is vital to check that there are no feelings of resentment or hidden agendas within the team.

It could be useful to start a discussion by asking 'Do we all agree that this is the best option?' If anyone disagrees or feels less than fully committed, it is the duty of the team to discuss the issue and persuade him or her that the chosen option is indeed the best option. This may often involve getting the other team members to explain the reasons why they chose the option that they prefer. For example, one option may stand out because of budget or other resource constraints, or it may be the least risky. Whatever the reasons, it is important to explain these to people who feel uncommitted so that they **buy in** to the final option.

We've decided that we need to organise an advertising campaign to market our new brand of washing powder. But it's a big task – what should we do first?

Once you have decided on an option that deals with the team's mission, the team must undertake to act upon it. When taking on a large task or complex project, it is vital to **break it down into smaller chunks**.

The team must then **assign responsibilities** – in other words, each member of the team must take on a chunk of the work. The final step is to create an **action plan** that describes the actions that each member of the team must take. Writing up a plan helps to prevent misunderstandings at a later stage such as 'But I thought you were going to do that!'

The steps to action planning are as follows:

- Get the team to think about the steps involved in doing the task.

- Once the team has decided on the various steps, ask the group to decide when each step should be done by. For example, one task may need to be completed before another can begin.

- Think about the resources (money, people, information) that may be needed to complete each step.

- Check that everyone understands what is involved at each step.

- Then ask for a volunteer to take on the specific action. If no one volunteers, ask the team to suggest the best person to do it – but always give people the option not to take on a particular action if they have a good reason not to.

- Finally, check that each member of the team has an approximately equal workload – you don't want to unfairly burden just one or two members of the team and let others get away without much to do!

Creating a written plan prevents the team from being all talk and no action.

 MEASURING RESULTS

A team can easily convince itself that – just because its overall deadline is months or even years in the future – it has plenty of time to achieve its goal. Wrong!

A good team will **check its progress** at regular intervals against the action plan. At successive team meetings you should encourage people to **report back** to the rest of the team on what they have been doing. If any particular team members are not making progress, or have been held up in any way from completing their tasks, the team as a whole must decide on a course of action to **rectify** the situation.

Avoid telling off or blaming an individual – try to ask questions to understand how the delay arose. The following questions may help you to probe how to get the team back on track:

- What do we need to do to get things back on track?

- How can we make sure that this sort of delay doesn't happen to us again?

- Are there any other tasks on our action plan that are affected because of this delay?

- Do we need to amend the action plan to make sure that we still reach our overall objective/deadline?

What gets measured, gets done.

Making what matters work for you

✔ Harness the energy and enthusiasm of the team by defining a single clear purpose, its mission statement. A team with ambiguous goals will never know when it has reached them.

✔ Use brainstorming to generate ideas as to how to achieve the team's purpose. Don't worry about the quality of these ideas for the moment and don't ignore the 'obvious' ideas as these can sometimes be the best ones.

✔ Think about the feasibility, pros and cons of each of the options to trim the list of ideas into a more manageable number.

✔ Decide what further information the team needs to gather before it can make a firm decision as to which option to pursue.

✔ Help the team to decide who needs to do what, how, and by when in order to fulfil the team's overall mission.

✔ Finally, keep track of how well (or badly) the team is performing. If the team is slipping against its action plan, help it to think of further actions to get back on schedule.

4 Managing Team Meetings

Team meetings can be a waste of time,
so make sure yours are not.

4

things that
really matter

1 **PREPARING FOR MEETINGS**

2 **ENCOURAGING PARTICIPATION**

3 **KEEPING THE DISCUSSION ON TRACK**

4 **MAINTAINING INTEREST**

Applying the teamworking process described in Chapter 3 will help a team to achieve its goals over the course of months or even years. However, a good team leader must **manage each meeting effectively**. A good meeting must meet the needs of all the members of the team – but it needn't be boring! To start with, doing a few minutes of advance **preparation** will help you make the best use of meeting time and maintain people's energy levels.

As the team's leader, it's important not to use your experience or position to bulldoze the team into making decisions that they don't agree with. Instead, you need to use your expertise to **guide** the team to come up with **solutions that everyone agrees with.**

The theory of teamworking is easy – it's the practice of handling team members that's the difficult bit!

IS THIS YOU?

● *We quite often waste time in meetings deciding what to talk about in the meeting.* ● *The team just doesn't seem that interested in being there – people are often having their own little side discussions.* ● *We sometimes discuss matters that really only require the Marketing Manager, Marketing Assistant and myself to attend. What should I do with the other four people on the team?* ● *I get so frustrated because David always talks over other people in team meetings.* ● *Our meetings sometimes last for three hours and I can tell that people get a bit bored.* ● *We have a lot of material to cover. Is there any way to get more done in the same amount of time?* ● *Matt is quite shy and obviously very nervous about speaking up in a group – are there any techniques I can use to encourage his participation?*
● *We quite often run over time on meetings.*

 PREPARING FOR MEETINGS

A lot of time is often wasted in meetings because there is no clearly stated purpose to them. For instance, team members may not have the right documents to hand if they didn't think that they would need them. Or people may not have completed a particular task because they didn't think the deadline was until the end of the week.

Consequently, some team leaders find it useful to set an agenda for each meeting. You may not find it necessary to be so formal, but there is certainly benefit in spending a little time preparing before each meeting.

A good team leader will try to **contact** team members to speak to each individual **before** each meeting. You will probably work on a daily basis with many of the people on your team, so all you need to do is to spend a few minutes talking to them about the upcoming team meeting. For the people that you do not encounter regularly, try to catch up with them briefly – perhaps by giving them a quick telephone call.

In order to create the agenda, you might want to ask them some of the following questions, as relevant:

- What issues do we need to discuss in the meeting?

- Is there any information that you need to tell the others?

- What do you personally need to get out of the meeting to feel that it had been a good use of your time?

- What is the one most important thing that we must achieve by the end of the meeting?

Contacting people ahead of the meeting is also a good – and subtle – way to remind people that there is a meeting coming up.

Once you have spoken to as many of the team members as you can, try to spend some time thinking through how you will manage the meeting:

- How will you set the scene?

- Which topics are you going to discuss?

- How much time do you want to allocate to each topic for discussion?

Managing meetings isn't rocket science – it just requires a little forward planning.

 ENCOURAGING PARTICIPATION

You're the team leader for a reason. You may be more senior or have greater understanding of the issues that the team is facing. Whatever the reason, you might sometimes feel under pressure to come up with the answers. It can be easy for the members of the team to rely on you for the solutions to all of their problems. However, this is not the way for teams to perform well!

If you were a team member, wouldn't you rather work towards a goal that you had contributed to, rather than one that your boss had dumped on you? So, rather than using your skills or expertise to provide solutions for the team, you should be encouraging the team to come up with its own solutions. It's about **guiding and supporting** the team in tackling problems, not directing and bossing people about.

Consequently, try to encourage people to contribute by using some of the following tactics:

- **Ask open-ended questions** to everyone in the team. For example, 'What does everyone feel about that?' or 'How can we achieve this?'

- **Respond positively** to contributions made by members of the team. For example, you could use phrases such as 'Good point', 'Thank you for that', or 'That's a good idea'. This will encourage people who make good suggestions.

- **Use further questions to probe for more detail**. For example, 'That's a good idea – what do you mean by that exactly?' or 'Could you just explain that in a bit more detail please?'

- **Give members of the team time to think**. If you are stood up at the front of the room, even a few seconds can feel like a long time. Sometimes, team members need a few moments of silence to put their thoughts into words. So when you ask a question, hold back and try to avoid answering it yourself.

- **Ask for different points of view.** 'What does anyone else think about that?' 'Can anyone see any problems with that suggestion?'

- **Remind everyone that they are all members of the team.** The responsibility for achieving the team's mission falls as much on their shoulders as it does on yours. As team leader, your job is to help the team to achieve the mission that everyone had agreed on, not give them orders to achieve your own personal mission!

- **Give extra consideration to naturally shy or junior team members.** Using someone's name can help to draw them out. For example saying 'James, do you agree with what we've been saying' may elicit a reaction. And when a quieter person does make a contribution, be certain to acknowledge it – for instance by writing it up or saying 'good point'. However, be careful not to embarrass a quiet person or you will make it twice as unlikely that he or she will contribute in the future.

- **Watch your body language.** Make sure that your body language – your face, posture, arms, etc – reinforce the words that are coming out of your mouth. For instance, watch out that you don't frown at suggestions that you don't agree with.

- **Avoid disagreeing with statements too strongly.** When you find fault with a statement or disagree strongly with something that has just been said, avoid saying 'you're wrong'. This will give the impression that – as the team leader – you know best. Instead, try to ask other members of the team what they think. Good phrases to use include 'Does everyone agree with that?' or 'That's a valid point of view. Does anyone else feel differently about that?' Only if no one speaks up should you add in your thoughts.

A good leader collaborates with their team to come up with the best ways forward.

 KEEPING THE DISCUSSION ON TRACK

A common complaint is that a meeting can go on for hours, yet fail to cover all of the important issues that need discussing. It's your job to watch the clock and keep the discussion focused on what the team **needs to do**.

At times, particular team members can have strong opinions and try to **dominate** the discussion. Or they may insist on talking about a particular issue in too much detail. When this does happen, it can be very difficult for anyone else to get a word in edgeways!

When someone does talk too much, you could try to:

- **Use your body language** to close him or her down. For example, if you are already on your feet, try standing further away from the dominating person. Another subtle way to discourage someone from talking too much is to **avoid** making too much **eye contact** with the dominating person.

If the subtle approach to closing someone down does not work, try using a more direct approach:

- Thank the person for their contribution. After all, you don't want to offend them and stop them from contributing further in the future.

- Explain the need to move on. For example, you could use a phrase such as, 'I'm conscious of the time and we still have a lot to do. Can we move the discussion on please?'

Another common problem is for team members to waste time **chatting** or **having side discussions** when the rest of the team is trying to discuss a serious topic. You could try to:

- Use physical movement to break up a side discussion. If you are already on your feet, you could stand near the people who are talking. Chances are that they will stop talking and pay attention to the rest of the team!

An alternative approach to stopping side discussions would be to have a frank discussion with the few team members who are not paying attention:

- Wait for the next convenient break – for example when the team wants to stop for a coffee or lunch – to have a quiet discussion with the people who are disrupting the team meeting.

- Ask them if they realise that their conversation is having a negative effect on the rest of the team.

- Ask them how they will behave in team meetings from now on.

While some people need to be encouraged to contribute, others need to be discouraged from contributing too much!

 MAINTAINING INTEREST

Lots of people hate meetings! How often have you heard someone say 'We've got a boring team meeting coming up this afternoon' or 'Not another meeting!'

However, meetings do not *have* to be boring! Here are just a few ways to liven up your meetings.

Syndicate group work

This is a common technique when a team is faced with two or more issues to discuss at once. The idea is that you divide the team up into two separate groups to cover an issue each. After a period of discussion in the separate syndicate groups, each syndicate then nominates someone to present the findings back to the combined team.

For example, if your team is faced with two decisions to make – choosing a new IT supplier and finding a venue for the Christmas party – you could split the team into two syndicates. Give them 45 minutes to discuss the issue and write up some notes on a sheet of flip chart paper. Warn them that each syndicate will have to give a five or ten minutes presentation of their findings back to the combined team.

After each syndicate has presented, facilitate a team discussion to see whether the people in each syndicate agree with the other group's suggestion.

Pair work

This is an extension of syndicate group work. Rather than splitting the team into two groups, you can divide the team up into pairs (if you have an uneven number of people on your team, you might want to sit out of the pair work). This is useful when the team has to cover a lot of ground in a short space of time.

Each pair can discuss an issue, problem or part of a topic, and then share their preliminary findings with the rest of the team. Again, it's useful for each pair to write up some of their initial thoughts on a sheet of flip chart paper.

Roving brainstorm

This is a useful technique for getting all members of the team involved. If you have a number of issues to cover in a meeting, write each of these up on a sheet of flip chart paper. Use Blu-tack to put them up on the walls of a room, then give each team member a pen. Ask everyone to move around the room, writing their suggestions as to how to tackle each issue on the sheets of paper. After a period of time, say 20 minutes or half-an-hour, you can then go round the room, asking people to talk through their suggestions. Use the flip chart suggestions to prompt further discussion and to generate actions if necessary.

The roving brainstorm is especially useful after lunch – to prevent that post-lunch sleepiness that people often suffer!

When it is not possible to use any of the more exciting techniques you can still:

- **Watch out for energy levels in the team** and convene breaks when appropriate. If, for example, you sense that people in the team are getting tired, convene a coffee break. Use your initiative – if the team is being really unproductive, ask whether it would make sense to end the meeting for the day and to pick up another time.

- **Ask for volunteers to lead team meetings.** It can provide a refreshing change of pace for team members to hear someone other than you talking. You could either ask for someone to lead a part of a meeting or all of it. Make sure that if someone does lead some of the discussion that you support them – don't criticise their performance in front of the rest of the team. If you have any constructive criticisms, offer them to the volunteer in private, along with praise for whatever was good about their performance.

Use your initiative and imagination to create activities and exercises that will energise and involve your team.

MAKING WHAT MATTERS WORK FOR YOU

✔ Spend just a few minutes preparing before each meeting. Ask yourself what you and the other members of the team need to bring to the meeting. What are the vital topics that you need to cover? Do you need to set an agenda?

✔ Make sure that every person in your team feels comfortable speaking. Use verbal and non-verbal techniques to encourage contributions. Avoid using your seniority or greater experience to bulldoze the team into decisions!

✔ Keep a look out for the time. Meetings can fly by and the team may find that it has not actually achieved very much. Use subtle methods to close down people who are talking too much and to move the discussion on.

✔ Vary how you run meetings to keep people's interest up. Ask for volunteers to help you out. Or use syndicate groups, pair work, or the roving brainstorm to liven up meetings.

5 Supporting the Team

Most people can be great team players,
given the right support and development.

4

things that
really matter

1 **CREATING THE RIGHT CLIMATE**

2 **MOTIVATING THE TEAM**

3 **MONITORING TEAM PERFORMANCE**

4 **DEVELOPING THE TEAM**

Leading a team is about more than simply managing meetings well. Your job is to create the right climate – **a team environment** – in which people feel that they can speak honestly and that their contributions will be taken seriously.

You also need to motivate the team by **rewarding good teamworking** appropriately. However, be careful not to overdo it or you will end up *de*motivating your team.

Measuring team performance will give you an idea of how the team could improve. When you have identified which individuals need what sort of development, help them by **coaching** them on a one-to-one basis.

A team leader can't lead a team by simply dealing with issues that come up in the duration of team meetings – a team leader must invest some time and thought in developing the skills and spirit of the team.

IS THIS YOU?

● *Our most junior team member doesn't say much in meetings – I have a feeling he's afraid to speak up in front of his more experienced colleagues.* ● *I heard one team member criticising another behind her back, but I don't know if it's enough of a big deal to speak to him about it.* ● *I've heard that rewards can motivate people to work harder, but what kind of rewards should I offer my team?* ● *Amelia is an excellent administrator but I get the feeling she's getting bored of her role on the team.* ● *Stephen is the most productive member of the team but doesn't seem motivated by money. I'd like to find some way of showing him that I really appreciate all his hard work.* ● *It's clear that we chose the wrong supplier a couple of weeks ago – how can we avoid making the same mistake again?* ● *Several people are really struggling with their work – how can I help them without doing their work for them?* ● *I want to point out mistakes that people have made but don't want to sound too critical or negative.*

 ## CREATING THE RIGHT CLIMATE

Creating the right environment or culture within the team is essential for helping to move from just norming to **performing outstandingly**.

As the team progresses over time, your role as leader requires that you:

● **Encourage honesty and openness** at all times. Members of the team should feel able to express important opinions candidly, even if it might be difficult for others to hear. Sometimes teams believe that it would be 'career-limiting' for them to challenge people more senior than themselves – such as yourself as the team leader. However, honesty is essential – otherwise there is a danger that poor work or unacceptable behaviours might go unchallenged. You should encourage team members to be honest, but tactful in doing so.

- **Forbid personal attacks on other team members** as they are unproductive and unnecessary. When someone on your team does attack another person, it's your job to make it clear that such comments will not be tolerated. When things go wrong, for example, team members should be encouraged to make only constructive comments on how the situation could be improved or avoided in future – rather than to highlight personal flaws in other people.

- **Remind the team of its mission.** Teams can be an opportunity for people to socialise and have fun – but ultimately the team has a purpose. Teams that get sidetracked can fail to meet their goals. Your job is to pull people back to the team mission to ensure that your team meets it.

- **Identify opportunities for people to improve their weaknesses** – not just work to their strengths. For example, one member of the team might be very good at administration, yet it is hardly challenging for that person to be given all of the administrative duties between team meetings. Your job as team leader is to ensure that people do not become bored. What tasks is the team member less good at? Can you suggest to the team that it gives them some more interesting and challenging tasks?

Encourage your team to follow these guidelines at all times – not just in team meetings, but in their day-to-day work too. For example, if you hear a team member 'bitching' about other team members behind their backs, try to put a stop to it immediately.

A strong team climate is one of the essentials of a performing team. A team without the right spirit will never get beyond the storming stage.

 MOTIVATING THE TEAM

Bonuses, reward schemes and flashy job titles can motivate many people to work harder. For example, many companies offer cash bonuses or vouchers for outstanding work. However, most people will not go that extra mile for just money. To truly motivate your team, make them feel that you truly value their work.

Team members who feel valued by their leader usually say that they need to feel that:

- **Their leader really listens** to them and considers their ideas. Work hard to ensure that you never dismiss anyone's suggestions out of hand.

- **They are doing challenging work** – as opposed to overly boring work or work that is so challenging that it is stressful. Listening is a key skill here too – whenever the team allocates tasks to individuals, try to check whether each person is happy with the work that they are given. If someone finds a task very boring, explain that someone has to do the 'boring' task and that, the next time, you will try to find someone else to do it. If a member of the team finds a task too stressful, encourage the team to offer whatever support and guidance it can to help the stressed individual.

In addition to listening to the needs of your team and providing them with interesting work, also reward good work appropriately. Rewards can take many forms, such as financial bonuses and incentives, prizes and awards. However, an often over-looked and under-rated 'reward' is to **provide verbal praise**. Saying 'That was a job well done – you should feel really proud of yourself' or something similar can often buoy someone up immensely.

Whenever offering rewards of any kind – whether financial or emotional – try to keep the following guidelines in mind:

- **Be judicious**. Giving out too many rewards or too much praise can devalue their power. A leader who says 'great work, well done' only occasionally for truly exceptional work is much more believable than one who says it all the time in relation to mediocre work.

- **Explain to all team members the link between performance and reward**. For example, is reward given out for effort (i.e. someone who tries hard but may not get many results) or for output (i.e. someone who may not necessarily try hard, but generates results)? If you are thinking about introducing a formal reward system, make sure that everyone on the team understands the 'rules' under which they might expect to receive a reward. When giving out praise, also make sure that it's **specific**. Rather than saying 'great work', explain, for example, 'That was great because you remained calm even when the customer was starting to get angry and you dealt with her very quickly.'

- **Tackle poor performance.** There is nothing as demoralising for someone who is working hard than to see someone else who's lazy and 'getting away with it'.

Rewards – whether tangible or not – have to be earned, and everyone has to understand how they are given out.

 ## MONITORING TEAM PERFORMANCE

It's a good idea at the end of each meeting to check with the team how useful the meeting was. You don't need to make a big deal out of it. Just explain that you want to make meetings more effective, so you're going to ask a few questions to see how useful the meeting was.

You could use some of the following questions (if appropriate):

- Did we achieve what we needed to achieve in this meeting?

- Did we spend too long on any topics?

- Did we not spend long enough on any of the issues we had to cover?

- Was the length of the meeting okay?

- Was the syndicate group work/pair work/roving brainstorm useful?

- How can we make our next meeting even more effective?

Some members of the team may not feel comfortable offering what they might see as criticisms of how you lead team meetings. So make sure that you tell the team that you will not be offended if anyone has constructive ideas on how you can all work together better.

Assessing how the team is doing will help the team to move from norming to performing.

 DEVELOPING THE TEAM

Sometimes a particular team member may continually fail to deliver what they have promised to do. Rather than discussing it in the team environment – which can be potentially embarrassing for the individual – it can make sense to discuss the reasons 'off line' in a one-to-one meeting. In team meetings it can sometimes be difficult for individual team members to express difficulties that they are experiencing.

It is important to take some action or else other members of the team who do work hard will start to ask themselves why they bother.

You could use the following guidelines to **coach** and provide **feedback** to the individual:

- Set up a one-to-one discussion with the team member.

- Explain that no one is perfect and that it is your job as team leader to help the team to meet its goals by coaching individuals when necessary.

- Ask the individual what they do well or not so well in contributing to the team's overall goal. Give the individual an opportunity to discuss any issues or problems.

- Then tell the individual what you think of their performance. However, make sure you are **specific** and provide evidence in the form of examples to support your arguments. Rather than saying, for example, 'you are too quiet', it is more helpful to cite situations when you noticed this happening and discuss its impact or lack of impact on others.

- Finally ask the individual to come up with ways of improving their performance.

Don't fall into the trap of assuming you know what's best for other people. Listen to them before putting across your point of view.

MAKING WHAT MATTERS WORK FOR YOU

✔ Encourage the members of your team to be honest and respectful of each other in working together. Dishonesty, suspicion and personal attacks are the enemies of successful teamworking.

✔ Understand that people are motivated by more than money or tangible rewards. Team members will work hard if they feel that they are listened to and that hard work is recognised and truly valued.

✔ Don't rest on your laurels if you think that team meetings seem to be going well. Keep getting feedback and suggestions from the team on how to make meetings even better.

✔ Use one-to-one discussions with each team member to develop their skills and confidence in a 'safe environment' away from the pressures of the team.

6 Demonstrating True Team Leadership

Leading a team is hard work, and these final skills are the hardest of all!

5 things that really matter

1 **IDENTIFYING INTERNAL CONFLICTS**

2 **RESOLVING INTERNAL CONFLICTS**

3 **DEALING WITH EXTERNAL ISSUES**

4 **FINISHING A GOOD JOB**

5 **ENHANCING YOUR LEADERSHIP SKILLS**

Leading a team isn't about being everybody's best friend. There are some difficult tasks that fall on your shoulders.

Sometimes you may need to **resolve conflicts** and personality clashes between team members. Outside of the team there will be times when problems or situations arise that you will need to deal with too. When time is short and there is no opportunity for the team to get together, you may need to take charge and **delegate** work to cope with a crisis.

Eventually, if the team you are leading has accomplished its original objective, you should take the time to celebrate your success and **disband the team** so that the members can move on to new challenges.

Finally, you need to **appraise your own performance** and work on improving your team leadership skills. A great leader will never assume that he or she has 'made it'!

Leading a team is not just about handling issues within team meetings well – it's about dealing with issues outside of meetings too.

IS THIS YOU?

● *Our team keeps getting bogged down in disagreements.* ● *I get the feeling that members of the team compete for my attention and I'm not sure that it's a good thing.* ● *David and Ruth just don't seem to get on – they've started to snipe and argue in almost every meeting.* ● *I just heard that our company is being taken over! How does it affect my team's objectives?* ● *We have a crisis on our hands and our next team meeting isn't for two weeks. Help!* ● *I don't know what my team thinks of me – do they think I'm a good leader or not?* ● *I'm worried that other people in our organisation may not see me as an effective leader.* ● *I think I'm a pretty good team leader but there's always room for improvement.*

Ⓘ IDENTIFYING INTERNAL CONFLICTS

It's unrealistic to expect everyone to agree with each other all the time – in fact it's not even desirable. A team that does not experience the occasional dispute is unlikely to come up with many new ideas.

However, disagreements that linger can divert attention from the work at hand. Consequently, one of the most important challenges that leaders face is the **constructive resolution of conflicts** within the team.

Conflict can often arise as a cause of two broad categories of issues:

Content issues

Disagreements between team members because they strongly believe in their different points of view. For example, they may be basing their decision on different facts from each other. Or they might have different opinions on how best to move forward even though they may have the same information.

Personal issues

Antagonism between team members for personal reasons. One team member might not like or trust another team member. Or perhaps a team member resents the fact that someone else on the team has been promoted while they haven't. Personal issues often give rise to strong emotions such as anger, jealousy, distrust and dissatisfaction and must be handled very carefully.

People have a natural tendency to ignore conflict or put off dealing with it. Your job is to identify conflict as soon as possible to prevent a performing team from falling back into the storming phase.

 ## RESOLVING INTERNAL CONFLICTS

Here are some tips for dealing with each resulting type of conflict:

Content conflict

- First ensure that the two parties involved have **the same information**. For example, if one team member does not have all the data that another member has, there is obviously going to be scope for disagreement.

- When it is a matter of differing opinion rather than

different facts, try to **involve the rest of the team** in the discussion. Encourage the disagreeing team members to listen to the thoughts of the rest of the team and ask them whether they will abide with the decision that might arise out of the team discussion.

● Sometimes, it may be you that gets involved in a protracted disagreement with a member of the team as well. In such circumstances, follow the same guidelines and **ask the rest of the team** which direction to take. If the team decides to go against you, try to abide by their decision.

Personal conflict

● Have an 'off line' discussion with each of the warring individuals. Invite them to a one-to-one meeting with yourself to **discuss the conflict** and diagnose what the issues seem to be.

● Begin by telling each person what you perceive to be the issue. However, always approach personal conflicts with a high degree of **sensitivity and empathy**. Both parties involved can often feel that they have been wronged. Avoid using the word 'you' when you discuss the conflict with the individuals involved and instead try to use the word 'I'. For example, rather than saying '*you* keep sniping at Nick', try saying '*I* get the feeling that you and Nick don't get along.' Starting your sentences with 'I' makes it a less contentious statement than 'you' which can sound accusatory.

● Then ask the person for **their comments on the situation**. For example, after saying, 'I get the impression that . . .', you could ask, 'Is this a fair perception?'

- Try to **emphasise common ground** between the two parties concerned. For example, if a team member says 'I don't like him – he's been to business school and has these silly management ideas', try to find some common ground such as 'But you've both been in this company for five years now.'

- When you have had these discussions with each of the individuals concerned, ask each person to **commit to some action or behaviour**. As another example of using 'I' rather than 'you', rather than saying 'Will *you* stop putting Nick down?' you could perhaps ask 'What could *I* do to make things work better between the two of you?'

Dealing with conflict is one of the toughest – but most important – roles of a true team leader.

 DEALING WITH EXTERNAL ISSUES

Your job as leader includes filtering all sorts of external issues that might affect your team. For example, you might find that your organisation decides to merge with another organisation. Or your manager may get fired suddenly – leaving you and your team adrift!

Under such circumstances, you need to **investigate what it means for your team** and **communicate** the impact of such changes to the members of your team:

- **Investigate** the impact on your team. Ask the relevant people how any changes will affect your team. It might, for example, be worth asking how it affects your budget and resources, deadlines, and members of the team.

- **Communicate** the consequences of the changes to your team. If the consequences are not urgent, you could wait until the next team meeting. If urgent action is required, you may need to convene a meeting earlier than planned.

- **Decide** what action to take. Give your team the opportunity to discuss the changes and agree what your next steps should be.

Sometimes time may be so short that you need to take immediate action. The computer system may crash. A customer might phone with an unexpected and urgent request. You may need to deal with such problems immediately – you may not have the time to convene a team meeting to decide what to do. When immediate action is required, it is sometimes necessary to **delegate** work to one or two members of the team to get things done.

Here are the basic rules of effective delegation:

- **Be clear** in your own mind exactly what needs doing before you try to explain it to someone else.

- **Choose someone** to do it. Find out who is available and who is the best suited to the task.

- **Define the assignment** to the member of your team. Explain what you would like them to do, and be specific in defining when you need it done by. If necessary, apologise for the short notice and explain the circumstances leading to the problem.

- **Check** that they have the same **understanding** of the situation as you. In a crisis you may not be as clear as you would like to be – and the last thing you need now is a misunderstanding!

Finally, when the crisis has passed, make sure that you raise the issue at the next team meeting to discuss it thoroughly and **review** how the team coped with the situation.

A leader must learn to recognise when to let a team make decisions and when they need to take charge.

 FINISHING A GOOD JOB

The final stage of teams is **mourning**. While the name may imply that this is a bad thing, it is actually frequently a necessary step to complete the team cycle. When a team is set up to achieve a particular and finite objective, it just doesn't make sense to keep the team together when the job is done. It might seem like quite good fun to keep it together for a while longer – but ultimately people would start to get bored and restless. People need new challenges to move on to.

As team leader, you should review the successes of the project by completing a **project debrief**. Congratulate the team for a job well done. Then gather the team together – perhaps just for a half-hour session – and try to draw out the lessons the team has learned from working together. The following questions may help you get started:

- What went well about the way we worked together?

- What new skills have you learned in achieving our objectives?

- What was the least enjoyable thing about working on this team? How could we avoid this on a future team?

- If you are asked to join a new team in the future, what advice will you give the members of that team?

Teams aren't just about hard work – they're also about celebrating success. It's time to have a good night out!

 ENHANCING YOUR LEADERSHIP SKILLS

Good leaders learn from new situations and pick up new skills all the time. Whether you are leading an ongoing team or moving from project team to project team, you need to assess your skills and look for ways to develop yourself.

There are three basic ways to find out how you are doing as a leader:

- **Question yourself.** Ask yourself whether the team is working together as effectively as you would like. If not, why not?

- **Get feedback from the team.** Tell the people on your team that you are trying to improve how you lead the team and ask them for their honest opinions on what you do well and not so well.

- **Get feedback from people outside the team.** Other people in your organisation will have contact with the members of your team, and they will also have seen the results of what your team does or does not achieve. So they will also have an opinion on what you do well or not so well.

Once you have assessed your own development needs, take the time to think about what you can actually do to lead your team more effectively. It may help to think about the following questions when you are putting together your own **development plan**:

- What do I want to achieve?

- What steps will I take to achieve it?

- When will I do it by?

- How will I measure whether I have achieved it or not?

And when you've achieved everything on your development plan, go through the process again! Circumstances change and you need to ensure that you are equipped with all the skills that you need to lead an effective team.

Assume that you are doing a good job of leading the team at your peril. Paying attention to your own development needs as a leader shows your team the importance of learning and growth.

MAKING WHAT MATTERS WORK FOR YOU

✔ Be on the look out for personality clashes and conflicts within the team. Of all the problems that can hit a team, these are the most damaging.

✔ Take it upon yourself to take action to deal with conflicts at the earliest opportunity possible. Don't procrastinate and hope that the problem will go away! Problems that at first only seem trivial can easily snowball into irretrievable situations if you're not careful.

✔ Watch out for issues in the rest of the organisation that could affect your team's goals and its ability to meet those goals. If issues crop up, communicate them to your team. If emergencies occur, delegate and deal with them immediately.

✔ Don't let teams die a slow death. Debrief the team on the lessons it has learned, then go and celebrate your successes!

✔ Take the time to think about your own development. Are you the most effective leader you could be? If not, what could you be doing better?